W9-ACK-265

SNOWBOARD

by Joseph Gustaitis

Words that are defined in the glossary are in **bold** type the first time they appear in the text.

A table of abbreviations used for the names of countries appears on page 32.

Crabtree editor: Adrianna Morganelli
Proofreader: Crystal Sikkens
Editorial director: Kathy Middleton
Production coordinator and prepress technician: Katherine Berti
Developed for Crabtree Publishing Company by RJF Publishing LLC (www.RJFpublishing.com)
Editor: Jacqueline Laks Gorman
Designer: Tammy West, Westgraphix LLC
Photo Researcher: Edward A. Thomas
Indexer: Nila Glikin

Photo Credits:
Associated Press: Wide World Photos: p. 22
Corbis: Arno Balzarini/epa: p. 28; Erin Patrice O'Brien: p. 4
Getty Images: p. 7, 11, 12, 17, 21, 26, 27; AFP: p. 6, 8, 9, 14, 19; Sports Illustrated: p. 2, 10, 16, 18, 20, 24
Landov: Martin Schutt/dpa: front cover
Wikipedia: Arnold C (Buchanan-Hermit): p. 29

Cover: Shaun White (USA) during halfpipe competition at the 2006 Olympics.

CONTENTS

Library and Archives Canada Cataloguing in Publication

Gustaitis, Joseph Alan, 1944-
    Snowboard / Joseph Gustaitis.

(Winter Olympic sports)
Includes index.
ISBN 978-0-7787-4026-1 (bound).--ISBN 978-0-7787-4045-2 (pbk.)

    1. Snowboarding--Juvenile literature. 2. Winter Olympics--Juvenile literature. I. Title. II. Series: Winter Olympic sports

GV857.S57G88 2009   j796.939   C2009-903213-9

Library of Congress Cataloging-in-Publication Data

Gustaitis, Joseph Alan, 1944-
    Snowboard / Joseph Gustaitis.
        p. cm. -- (Winter Olympic sports)
    Includes index.
    ISBN 978-0-7787-4045-2 (pbk. : alk. paper)
    -- ISBN 978-0-7787-4026-1 (reinforced library binding : alk. paper)
    1. Snowboarding. I. Title.

    GV857.S57G87 2010
    796.939--dc22

                                    2009021494

Crabtree Publishing Company
www.crabtreebooks.com   1-800-387-7650

| **Published in Canada**
Crabtree Publishing
616 Welland Ave.
St. Catharines, ON
L2M 5V6 | **Published in the United States**
Crabtree Publishing
PMB16A
350 Fifth Ave., Suite 3308
New York, NY 10118 | **Published in the United Kingdom**
Crabtree Publishing
White Cross Mills
High Town, Lancaster
LA1 4XS | **Published in Australia**
Crabtree Publishing
386 Mt. Alexander Rd.
Ascot Vale (Melbourne)
VIC 3032 |

AN INTRODUCTION TO SNOWBOARD

Snowboard is a combination of exciting sports. It is like skiing because it's done on snow but also like surfing and skateboarding because it's done on a board.

Philipp Schoch (SUI) in action during the men's parallel giant slalom at the 2006 Winter Games.

OLYMPICS FACT FILE

THE EARLY DAYS

In Minnesota in 1917, a man named Vern Wicklund invented a snowboard made from boards taken from a barrel. The sport didn't catch on, however, until the 1960s. That's when a Michigan engineer named Sherman Poppen invented a simple snowboard called the Snurfer (combining the words "snow" and "surfer"). The original was made from a child's skis screwed together, with a rope attached to the front. Poppen sold a lot of Snurfers, but many people thought they were just toys. Then young fans of the Snurfer started making and selling high-quality snowboards — which were not toys anymore.

THE RIGHT GEAR

Besides the right snowboard, a snowboarder also needs boots (hard or soft, depending on the event), bindings, and gloves. Not all snowboarders wear helmets, but they are a good idea.

- The Olympic Games were first held in Olympia, in ancient Greece, around 3,000 years ago. They took place every four years until they were abolished in 393 A.D. A Frenchman named Pierre Coubertin (1863–1937) revived the Games, and the first modern Olympics — which featured only summer sports — were held in Athens in 1896.

- The first Olympic Winter Games were held in 1924 in Chamonix, France. The Winter Games were then held every four years except in 1940 and 1944 (because of World War II), taking place in the same year as the Summer Games, until 1992.

- The International Olympic Committee decided to stage the Summer and Winter Games in different years, so there was only a two-year gap before the next Winter Games were held in 1994. They have been held every four years from that time.

- The symbol of the Olympic Games is five interlocking colored rings. Together, they represent the union of the five regions of the world — Africa, the Americas, Asia, Europe, and Oceania (Australia and the Pacific Islands) — as athletes come together to participate in the Games.

FROM REBELS TO OLYMPIANS

Snowboard isn't just for **mavericks** anymore! Since 1998, it has been a popular part of the Winter Olympics.

Ross Powers (USA), a 2002 gold medalist, with one of his boards.

AN "OUTSIDER" SPORT

In snowboard's early days, fans saw it as a sport for rebels and outsiders, with an "edgy" image. Snowboard makers put wild designs on the boards. Most ski areas banned snowboarders, seeing them as kids with bad attitudes who might injure skiers with their dangerous moves. By the 1990s, after snowboard instructors became organized and snowboard became a **professional** sport, nearly all ski resorts lifted the ban.

INVENTING THE HALFPIPE

In the 1970s, skateboarders learned to do tricks on something called a **halfpipe**. This is a smooth U-shaped structure that looks like a big pipe or tube cut in half. In the early 1980s, some young snowboarders at Lake Tahoe, California, created a snowboard halfpipe out of a natural gully. One of them, Terry Kidwell, is often thought of as the creator of halfpipe freestyle snowboard.

SNOWBOARD HITS EUROPE

In the 1980s, European visitors to the United States began bringing snowboards back home. By 1990, most European ski resorts allowed snowboards. Some of them even began building halfpipes.

LEARN THE LINGO

Snowboarders have created their own colorful language. Here are some examples:

Airdog—a snowboarder who does high jumps
Fakie—riding backward
Gnarly—really good
Tognar—totally gnarly
Shralp—riding really hard
Biff—wiping out on a fall

THE OLYMPICS

Snowboard was a **demonstration sport** at the 1994 Winter Olympics. Four years later, snowboard became a full Olympic sport with two events, halfpipe and giant slalom. The events have been changed a bit in the Olympics as the years went on.

WHAT'S IN A SNOWBOARD?

Snowboards look like a wide ski. They have a wooden core, with layers of **fiberglass** and plastic added around. A strip of steel, called the edge, is attached. The edge helps the rider make turns on the board.

THE OLYMPIC EVENTS

Three exciting events are featured in snowboard—parallel giant slalom, halfpipe, and snowboard cross. There are men's and women's competitions in all three.

Crispin Lipscomb (CAN) soars high above the halfpipe during the 2006 Olympic Games.

PARALLEL GIANT SLALOM

Two boarders go head-to-head in this race. They zigzag down the mountain, racing as they turn through a series of gates. The idea is to go as fast as you can without falling.

HALFPIPE

This is the event for the snowboarders who like to show off! Halfpipe began when snowboarders tried to imitate the tricks that skateboarders do. One boarder at a time goes down the halfpipe, doing all kinds of stunts and tricks. Judges decide who is the best.

SNOWBOARD CROSS

Snowboard cross first came to the Olympics in 2006. Four racers go down the course at a time, speeding down the mountain while also dealing with bumps, big jumps, and sharp turns on the course. The event is exciting to watch because of all the jumps and the chance of crashes. Sometimes one racer tries to pass another racer while in midair.

MORE EVENTS

There are five events at the snowboard World Championships and other international competitions—parallel slalom, parallel giant slalom, halfpipe, snowboard cross, and **big air**.

DID YOU KNOW?

Because the snowboard events are so different, most of the top snowboarders compete in only one of the three Olympic competitions.

OOPS!

Falls are common in snowboard. When a racer falls, it's called a **wipe-out**.

THE 2010 OLYMPICS

Snowboard competition at the Vancouver 2010 Olympics will be held at Cypress Mountain. Existing ski runs were renovated, and a new halfpipe and parallel giant slalom course were built.

Action during the women's snowboard cross competition, 2006.

7

PARALLEL GIANT SLALOM

It's boarder versus boarder in this exciting race
on a mountain that's full of trouble.

*Karine Ruby (FRA), during the routine
that won her a 2002 silver medal in
women's parallel giant slalom.*

SUPER STATS

Switzerland has won the most medals in giant slalom and parallel giant slalom, with five—three gold, one silver, and one bronze. France is next with three medals, including two gold and one silver.

Switzerland's Philipp (right) and Simon Schoch go for gold and silver in men's parallel giant slalom, 2006.

OLYMPIC CHANGE

The parallel giant slalom was first done at the Winter Olympics in 2002. At the 1998 Games, the event was known simply as the giant slalom, and boarders came down the mountain one at a time. They were timed by a clock and the fastest racer won. In the parallel giant slalom, two boarders race on the mountain at the same time. The winner goes on to the next round of competition.

RUNNING THE RACE

The competition begins with **qualifying rounds**. Each racer gets two runs, one on the blue course and one on the red. The two times are added, and the top 16 snowboarders go on to the main competition. They go through several rounds until the final, where the two fastest riders face off.

DISQUALIFIED!

A boarder can be **disqualified** for missing a gate and not going back to do it again. A boarder can also be disqualified for not completing the course or for beginning the race before being given the signal to start.

THE COURSE

The parallel giant slalom has two courses side by side—a red one and a blue one. The drop in height from the top of the course to the bottom is 548 feet (167 m). The course is 1,690 feet (515 m) long.

SPECIAL BOOTS

Competitors in parallel giant slalom wear boots with a hard, stiff exterior, which provides the foot and ankle the support they need.

M'N'S PARALL'L
GIANT SLALOM

Two by two, boarders come speeding down the mountain,
jumping over bumps and carving sharp turns.

*Ross Rebagliati (CAN) winning the
gold medal in giant slalom in 1998.*

KING OF THE MOUNTAIN

Philipp Schoch (SUI) won the gold medals in the men's parallel giant slalom at both the 2002 and the 2006 Winter Games. His win in 2002 was considered an upset. Schoch beat Richard Richardsson (SWE), who had won the World Championship in 1999, when Richardsson raced wide of the gates and almost fell a couple of times.

THE FIRST GOLD MEDAL

Back in 1998—when the event was the giant slalom (with only one boarder racing at a time) — Ross Rebagliati (CAN) was the first winner of the Olympic gold medal. Rebagliati's time of 2.03:96 beat the second-place finisher, Thomas Prugger (ITA), by only two-hundredths of a second. Rebagliati had been winning championships since 1991, when he was the amateur snowboard champion in both Canada and the United States.

BACK FROM THE BRINK

Two years before the 2002 Winter Games, Chris Klug (USA) thought he had only a few months to live. He had a rare liver disease. Fortunately, he was able to get a liver transplant. He returned to snowboard and went on to win the bronze medal.

A DANGEROUS EVENT

The parallel giant slalom can be dangerous. Snowboarder Daniel Loetscher (SUI) was killed during a race in Switzerland in 2000. He lost his balance and smashed into a pillar marking the finish line.

Chris Klug (USA), winning bronze in 2002.

WOMEN'S PARALLEL GIANT SLALOM

The women's parallel giant slalom features the same format as the men's — and just as many surprises.

Daniela Meuli (SUI) celebrates her 2006 victory in the women's parallel giant slalom.

DON'T MAKE MISTAKES

When Daniela Meuli (SUI) won the gold medal at the 2006 Winter Olympics, she had a little help from her competitors, who made costly mistakes. In the semifinal race, Rosey Fletcher (USA) had a slight lead over Meuli after the first run. In the second run, however, Fletcher fell. In the final round, Amelie Kober (GER) seemed to be pulling ahead of Meuli, but then Kober crashed into the safety fence. Meuli made no mistakes and came in first.

SO CLOSE

Doris Guenther (AUT) placed fourth in the women's parallel giant slalom in 2006, just missing the **podium**. She also competed in snowboard cross in the 2006 Games, winding up in 14th place.

DID YOU KNOW?

In parallel giant slalom, there are complicated rules to break ties in all the rounds of competition except the final medal round. In case of a tie in the medal round, both athletes receive the same color medal.

TWO-MEDAL WINNER

The first woman to win an Olympic gold medal in the women's giant slalom in 1998 was Karine Ruby (FRA), who won the race during a heavy snowfall. Four years later, Ruby won a silver medal in the parallel giant slalom. She is the only woman snowboarder to win two Olympic medals. Sadly, Ruby died in a mountain climbing accident in May 2009.

IT HELPS TO LIVE ON THE MOUNTAIN

Isabelle Blanc (FRA), who won the gold in the women's parallel giant slalom in 2002, got an early start in winter sports. When she was seven, her parents took over the management of a hotel at a famous French ski resort, where Isabelle quickly learned to ski. She then discovered the snowboard and went on to Olympic fame.

TRY, TRY, AGAIN

When Rosey Fletcher (USA) came to the 2006 Winter Games, it was her third Olympics. She had not won a medal because she had fallen in both previous Games. This time, however, she stayed on her feet in the final and won the bronze medal. She was the first American to win an Olympic medal in the women's parallel giant slalom.

Markku Koski (FIN) rides the board during the men's halfpipe finals in 2006.

HALFPIPE

With its tricks, spins, and jumps, halfpipe—which has been in the Olympics since 1998—is probably the most exciting snowboard event.

BOARDING THE HALFPIPE

Boarders begin their routine by dropping down one wall of the halfpipe. When they go up the other wall, they do a trick. They usually do six to eight tricks as they go through the halfpipe. The boarders do twists, flips, and spins and grab their boards as they soar. They try to go as high as they can. Form is also important.

JUDGING

Five judges decide the winner of a halfpipe competition. They each give a score of up to ten points. Judges must consider the height, difficulty, and variety and execution of the moves, plus how well they are done. Points are deducted for falls or other mistakes. Judging is hard because boarders are always inventing new tricks. Boarders are often unhappy with how the judges decide.

COMPETITION FORMAT

During qualifying rounds, each boarder does two runs. Only the better scoring run counts. The 12 boarders with the highest scores move on to the final. There, they also do two runs, with only the better run counting. The boarder with the highest score wins.

A LOT OF TRICKS

In halfpipe, Standard Airs are moves without rotation (twists and turns). Rotations are moves that do involve these spins. The most basic halfpipe move is the Alley-Oop, where the boarder makes a half-turn or more in the air. In a Straight Air, the boarder turns 180 degrees in the air while at the same time grabbing the board. In a Backside 720, the boarder makes two full turns in the air.

DID YOU KNOW?

If a halfpipe boarder makes a complete stop during his routine, the judges deduct two full points. If he falls but it doesn't stop or interrupt the routine, 1.6 to 1.9 points are deducted. There are specific point deductions for many other kinds of mistakes that halfpipe riders can make.

THE RIGHT BOARD

Halfpipe boards are short, wide, and flexible. The front and back ends are curved upward. The shape of the board makes it possible for the boarder to balance, do tricks, ride forward and backward, and take off and land in different directions.

BOOTS AND BINDINGS

Halfpipe boarders wear soft boots that provide foot and ankle support but let them move their feet around. The boots are strapped to the board with soft bindings.

MEN'S HALFPIPE

The United States has ruled the men's Olympic halfpipe competition with some fantastic performances.

Gold medal winner Shaun White (USA) in action during the 2006 halfpipe competition.

DOMINATION

Of the nine medals awarded in men's halfpipe since 1998, the United States has won six. At the 2002 Winter Games, the United States finished 1–2–3. At the 2006 Games, the United States finished 1–2–4.

HIGH HALFPIPE

Most halfpipes are 18 feet (5.5 m) or 22 feet (6.7 m) high. The halfpipe in the Olympics has 22-foot-high walls.

THE FLYING TOMATO

Because of his red hair, Shaun White (USA) has been called the "Flying Tomato." He began snowboarding when he was six and turned professional when he was 12. He grew up to be even better. White won the Olympic gold medal in 2006 at age 19 in what many people said was one of the greatest halfpipe performances ever delivered. He scored 46.8 out of a possible 50 points.

Danny Kass (USA), on the way to a silver medal in the 2006 halfpipe.

JERSEY GIANT

Most snowboarders come from places where there are a lot of mountains, like Colorado or Switzerland. Danny Kass (USA), however, comes from a surprising location—New Jersey—where he learned the sport. Coming from New Jersey didn't stop him from winning the silver medal twice—at the 2002 and the 2006 Winter Games.

FROM THIRD TO FIRST

Ross Powers (USA) won the bronze medal in 1998. Four years later, he came back to win the gold one day after his 23rd birthday. He did an amazing display of tricks. On some tricks, he flew 18 feet (5.5 m) above the pipe.

SILVER: DANNY KASS (USA)   BRONZE: MARKKU KOSKI (FIN)

WOMEN'S HALFPIPE

Hannah Teter (USA) in action during the women's halfpipe final at the 2006 Games.

Women from the United States have turned in some terrific performances in the halfpipe, with four Olympic medals, but Europeans have given them some stiff competition.

2006 OLYMPIC MEDALISTS: GOLD: HANNAH TETER (USA)

Nicola Thost (GER) in 1998, winning the first gold medal awarded in women's halfpipe.

HANNAH'S GOLD

Hannah Teter (USA) finished first in the women's halfpipe at the 2006 Olympics. Her family in Vermont has long been making maple syrup. Today, she makes and sells a maple syrup called Hannah's Gold. The money she makes goes to help children in a village in Kenya.

THE FIRST WINNER

Nicola Thost (GER) was the first boarder to win the gold medal in the women's halfpipe, in 1998. She then won the U.S. Open Snowboarding Championship halfpipe event two years in a row. In 2003, Thost retired from snowboard competition because of knee injuries.

KELLY'S McTWIST

Three days before the final halfpipe competition at the 2002 Winter Olympics, Kelly Clark (USA) got hurt. She was trying to do a difficult jump called the **McTwist**. She fell and laid on the snow for 20 minutes. She came to the finals with a sore back. On her final run down the pipe, she did seven tricks, including a perfect McTwist, and won the gold medal with a great score of 47.9 points.

MEDALS FOR NORWAY

Norway is the only country besides the United States to win more than one medal in the women's halfpipe at the Winter Games. Stine Brun Kjeldaas won the silver medal in 1998, and Kjersti Buaas won the bronze in 2006. Together, the two snowboarders have produced a series of snowboard shows for Norwegian television.

SILVER: GRETCHEN BLEILER (USA)   BRONZE: KJERSTI BUAAS (NOR)   19

SNOWBOARD CROSS

Snowboard cross is one of the newest sports in the Olympics. The event—in which four boarders race in a pack down the course—first came to the Games in 2006.

Four boarders leap during the men's snowboard cross competition in 2006.

DID YOU KNOW?

Boarders wear colored bibs that correspond to their position in the starting gate. The colors are black, yellow, red, and blue.

Canada's Maelle Ricker competes in the women's snowboard cross in 2006.

THE COURSE

A boarder who does snowboard cross has to speed down the mountain like a slalom racer and do jumps, almost like a halfpipe boarder. The straight jumps are called **kickers**, and the jumps on an angle are called **spines**. The course is marked by gates and has sharp banked turns and **moguls**, which are small, hard bumps on the slope. Going over a mogul makes the boarder fly into the air.

CROWD CONTROL

Because four boarders are racing at the same time and the course is narrow, crashes are a constant danger.

THE COMPETITION

The snowboard cross competition goes in stages. For the first two runs, boarders race against the clock. The 32 men and the 16 women with the best times then go on. The boarders then race in groups of four, and the top two racers in each **heat** move on through the next rounds. Finally, four boarders are left to race for the gold medal.

DON'T GET TOO CLOSE

Snowboard cross racers can get awfully close to one another. Sometimes one racer will even touch another racer on the back. But if a racer is too close and the competitor in front of her falls, she'll fall, too. Also, judges on the course watch to see if a boarder is tugging or pulling on another boarder, which is not allowed. Any boarder who purposely causes another racer to fall down, slow down, or leave the course is disqualified.

MEN'S SNOWBOARD CROSS

The best snowboarders haven't always won this event. Sometimes, a racer wins because he's the one who stays on his feet.

Seth Wescott (USA) races to a gold medal in the 2006 men's snowboard cross.

2006 OLYMPIC MEDALISTS: GOLD: SETH WESCOTT (USA)

HEART AND SOUL

In the gold medal race in men's snowboard cross at the 2006 Winter Games, Radoslav Zidek (SVK) looked like the winner. About three-fourths of the race had been run, and he was still leading Seth Wescott (USA). Then Wescott put on a burst of speed and soared into the air on the last jump. He passed Zidek and finished first by the length of just half a snowboard. After the race, Wescott said, "I think snowboarding is becoming the heart and soul of the Olympics."

THE FASTEST FALLS

Winning in snowboard cross is sometimes a matter of survival. Most people thought Drew Neilson (CAN) would win the snowboard cross at the 2006 Winter Olympics. On the last day of competition, he was the fastest qualifier during the morning runs. But five seconds after the start of his final race, Neilson was bumped by a rider behind him. Neilson rolled down the course and hurt himself. He wound up 17th.

BOOTS AND BINDINGS

Some snowboard cross competitors wear hard racing boots, but most wear softer boots — though stiffer than the boots used in halfpipe. The bindings used to attach the boots to the board depend on the type of boot.

TIE BREAKER

If two or more riders are tied at the end of the gold medal round, officials look at photos to see which rider's body or board crossed the finish line first. If there is still a tie, the rider with the fastest qualification time wins the race — and the gold medal.

TRAGEDY ON THE SLOPE

Snowboard cross can be extremely dangerous. Accidents can result in injury and even death. A month after finishing 12th at the 2006 Winter Olympics, Jonatan Johansson (SWE) was killed in a fall at Whiteface Mountain in Wilmington, N.Y. He was doing a warm-up run for a snowboard cross competition and took a hard fall on a jump.

THE RIGHT BOARD

The boards used in snowboard cross are long and stiff and capable of going at high speeds and in different directions. They are more like the boards used in halfpipe than those used in parallel giant slalom.

WOMEN'S SNOWBOARD CROSS

The women's snowboard cross competition might have a short Olympic history, but it has already had its share of exciting moments.

Lindsey Jacobellis (USA) wipes out at the end of the 2006 women's snowboard cross final, losing the gold medal.

LOSING AT THE LAST SECOND

Lindsey Jacobellis (USA) looked like a sure gold-medal winner in the women's snowboard cross at the 2006 Winter Olympics. She was sailing down the course with ease, well ahead of Tanja Frieden (SUI). Then Jacobellis lost her balance and fell just short of the finish line. Frieden sped past her and won the first Olympic gold medal in women's snowboard cross. Jacobellis ended up with the silver.

HER SECOND JOB

When she's not training for the Olympics, Dominique Maltais (CAN), who won the bronze medal in 2006, is a firefighter in Montreal, Canada.

NO HOT DOGS, PLEASE

In snowboard, you're **hot-dogging** if you do a trick during a race just to show off. A lot of people think these tricks add excitement to the sport, but hot-dogging can hurt. Some people think Lindsey Jacobellis (USA) lost the gold medal in 2006 because she was hot-dogging. On her next-to-last jump, Jacobellis grabbed her snowboard in a trick called a backside method grab. It cost her the gold.

OUCH!

In the final women's snowboard cross race at the 2006 Olympics, Maelle Ricker (CAN) took such a hard fall that she had to be flown by helicopter to a hospital. She was released from the hospital later that night. She ended up fourth in the competition. Ricker has also competed in the Olympics in halfpipe.

ONE TO WATCH

In January 2009, Helene Olafsen (NOR) won the gold medal in women's snowboard cross at the Snowboard FIS World Championship in Korea. When she trains for races, she likes to practice in the halfpipe. In 2006, Olafsen was only 16 years old and was competing in the World Junior Championships rather than the Olympics.

THE OTHER SIDE OF SNOWBOARD

For different reasons, a lot of great snowboarders never competed in the Winter Games. They've got many other snowboard events to enter!

Terje Haakonsen (NOR), one of the greatest snowboarders ever, at the 2002 Winter X Games.

Shaun White (USA) winning a gold medal at the 2009 Winter X Games.

THE BEST EVER?

Many people consider Terje Haakonsen (NOR) to be the greatest snowboarder ever. In the 1990s, he won the International Snowboarding Federation World Championships in halfpipe three times. He invented a famous halfpipe trick called the **Haakon flip**. In 2007, he set the record for "highest air," soaring 32 feet (9.8 m) above the halfpipe. Haakonsen didn't enter the Olympics in 1998. He thought the Games were too commercial, he didn't like the judging system, and he didn't want to wear a uniform.

A DIFFERENT EVENT

Janna Meyen-Weatherby (USA) is one of the top snowboarders in the world, but she doesn't compete in the Olympics. She specializes in **slopestyle** snowboard, which is not an Olympic event. In slopestyle, snowboarders race down a slope like in the slalom, but they also zoom down narrow rails and soar over large ramps, doing tricks in the air like in halfpipe.

THE ROCK STAR

When snowboard was in its early days and had its "outsider" image, Shaun Palmer (USA) was the star. Kids loved the wild designs on his snowboards and his outrageous clothes and hair. He was one of the greatest halfpipe riders ever.

THE WINTER X GAMES

The Winter X Games is a yearly event, usually held in January. It focuses on "extreme" sports. Some of them, like snowmobiling, are not done at the Olympics. Snowboarders do halfpipe and snowboard cross, but they also do slopestyle and big air—a competition that emphasizes high jumps into the air and aerial tricks—which are not Olympic events. Many athletes who participate in the Olympics also take part in the X Games.

A SNAPSHOT OF THE VANCOUVER 2010 WINTER OLYMPICS

SNOWBOARD
THE ATHLETES

Everyone is getting ready for Vancouver in 2010! Olympic teams are still being determined. The listings below include the top finishers in a selection of events in the 2008-2009 World Cup. Who among them will be the athletes to watch in the Vancouver Winter Olympics? Visit the Web site www.vancouver2010.com for more information about the upcoming competitions.

Kevin Pearce from the United States jumps to win the Halfpipe final at the Burton European Open Snowboarding Championships 2008 in Laax, Switzerland.

FIS SNOWBOARD WORLD CUP 2008–09

Men—Overall Standings:
1. Siegfried Grabner (AUT)
2. Markus Schairer (AUT)
3. Benjamin Karl (AUT)
4. Jasey Jay Anderson (CAN)
5. Andreas Prommegger (AUT)

Women—Overall Standings:
1. Doris Guenther (AUT)
2. Lindsey Jacobellis (USA)
3. Amelie Kober (GER)
4. Liu Jiayu (CHN)
5. Maelle Ricker (CAN), Janine Tischer (GER)

SNOWBOARD EVENTS

2009 World Snowboard Championships—Gangwon, Korea
Men—Halfpipe:
1. Ryoh Aono (JPN)
2. Jeff Batchelor (CAN)
3. Mathieu Crepei (FRA)

Women—Halfpipe:
1. Liu Jiayu (CHN)
2. Holly Crawford (AUS)
3. Paulina Ligocka (POL)

Men—Parallel GS:
1. Jasey Jay Anderson (CAN)
2. Sylvain Dufour (FRA)

3. Matthew Morison (CAN)
Women—Parallel GS:
1. Marion Kreiner (AUT)
2. Doris Guenther (AUT)
3. Patricia Kummer (SUI)

Men—Snowboard Cross:
1. Markus Schairer (AUT)
2. Xavier de le Rue (FRA)
3. Nick Baumgartner (USA)

Women—Snowboard Cross:
1. Helene Olafsen (NOR)
2. Olivia Nobs (SUI)
3. Mellie Francon (SUI)

THE VENUE IN VANCOUVER
CYPRESS MOUNTAIN

- venue capacity: 8,000
- located in Cypress Provincial Park, overlooking the city of Vancouver
- elevation: 3051 feet (930 m)

GLOSSARY

big air A competition that emphasizes aerial tricks and high jumps into the air

demonstration sport A sport that is played at the Olympics on a trial basis

disqualified To be eliminated from competition for not following the rules

fiberglass A strong, lightweight material often used in boats and cars

Haakon flip A halfpipe trick invented by Terje Haakonsen (NOR), in which the boarder takes off backward, does a somersault and two complete turns in the air, and lands going forward

halfpipe A snowboard structure shaped like a "U" or a tube cut in half; also the sport done on such a structure

heat One run down a course in a competition

hot-dogging Doing an unnecessary trick just to show off

kicker In snowboard cross, a straight jump

maverick Independent and not willing to conform to accepted views or attitudes

McTwist A snowboard trick in which the boarder turns $1\frac{1}{2}$ times in the air while grabbing the board in the middle, named for its inventor, Mike McGill

mogul A bump on a ski course

podium A platform on which the winners of an event stand

professional An athlete who is paid to play his or her sport

qualifying round A stage of competition that competitors must succeed at in order to move on to the next stage

slopestyle A type of snowboard competition in which the rider races down a slope while going down rails and over ramps, doing tricks in the air. Slopestyle is not done at the Olympics

spine In snowboard cross, a jump on an angle

wipe-out A crash or fall that happens while snowboarding

FIND OUT MORE

BOOKS

Cobb, Rosanne. *Skiing & Snowboarding: Everything You Need to Know About the Coolest Sports* (London: Collins & Brown, 2005)

Fitzpatrick, Jim. *Snowboarding* (Ann Arbor, MI: Cherry Lake Publishing, 2008)

Gifford, Clive. *Snowboarding: Learn to Snowboard Like a Pro* (New York: DK Publishing, 2007)

Kalman, Bobbie, and Kelley Macaulay. *Extreme Snowboarding* (St. Catharines, Ontario: Crabtree Publishing, 2004)

McNab, Neil. *Go Snowboard: Read It, Watch It, Do It* (New York: DK Publishing, 2006)

O'Neal, Claire. *Extreme Snowboarding with Lindsey Jacobellis* (Hockessin, DE: Mitchell Lane, 2008)

Slade, Suzanne. *Let's Go Snowboarding* (New York: PowerKids Press, 2007)

WEB SITES

ABC of Snowboarding   **www.abc-of-snowboarding.com**
A site that contains information on snowboard history, tips and tricks, and current events.

Canadian Snowboard Federation   **www.csf.ca**
The site of the organization overseeing snowboard in Canada.

International Olympic Committee   **www.olympic.org**
The official site of the International Olympic Committee, with information on all Olympic sports.

International Ski Federation   **www.fis-ski.com**
The site of the organization that oversees international and Olympic snowboard as well as all types of skiing.

United States of America Snowboard Association (USASA)   **www.usasa.org**
The site of the organization that governs all local and national amateur snowboard contests in the United States.

United States Ski and Snowboard Association   **www.ussa.org**
The site of the governing body for Olympic skiing and snowboarding in the United States.

INDEX

COUNTRY ABBREVIATIONS

AUT — Austria
CAN — Canada
FIN — Finland
FRA — France
GER — Germany
ITA — Italy
NOR — Norway
SUI — Switzerland
SVK — Slovakia
SWE — Sweden
USA — United States of America

Printed in the U.S.A. — CG